D0535875

THE LONG MEADOW

Winner of the 2003 James Laughlin Award
of The Academy of American Poets

The James Laughlin Award is given to commend and support a poet's second book. The only award of its kind in the United States, it is named in honor of the poet and publisher James Laughlin, who founded New Directions in 1936. The award is endowed by a gift to The Academy of American Poets from the Drue Heinz Trust.

Judges for 2003
Mary Jo Bang
Thom Gunn
Campbell McGrath

Also by Vijay Seshadri

Wild Kingdom

THE LONG MEADOW

Poems by
Vijay Seshadri

Graywolf Press
Saint Paul, Minnesota

Copyright © 2004 by Vijay Seshadri

Publication of this volume is made possible in part by a grant provided by the Minnesota State Arts Board, through an appropriation by the Minnesota State Legislature; a grant from the Wells Fargo Foundation Minnesota; and a grant from the National Endowment for the Arts. Significant support has also been provided by the Bush Foundation; Target, Marshall Field's and Mervyn's with support from the Target Foundation; the McKnight Foundation; and other generous contributions from foundations, corporations, and individuals. To these organizations and individuals we offer our heartfelt thanks.

MINNESOTA
STATE ARTS BOARD

NATIONAL
ENDOWMENT
FOR THE ARTS

Special funding for this title has been provided by the Jerome Foundation.

Published by
Graywolf Press
2402 University Avenue, Suite 203
Saint Paul, Minnesota 55114

All rights reserved.

www.graywolfpress.org

Published in the United States of America
Printed in Canada

ISBN 1-55597-400-7

2   4   6   8   9   7   5   3   1
First Graywolf Printing, 2004

Library of Congress Control Number: 2003112159

Cover art and design: Jeanne Lee

Acknowledgments

Grateful acknowledgment is made to the following periodicals—*Bomb* ("Wolf Soup"); *Lumina* ("North"); *The New Yorker* ("The Scholar," "The Disappearances," "The Long Meadow," "North of Manhattan," "Baby Baby"); *The Paris Review* ("Visiting Russia," "Interview," "Ailanthus"); *Poetry Daily* (on-line) ("Immediate City"); *Triquarterly* ("Anima," "Thelma"); *Western Humanities Review* ("Witch Elegy"); *The Yale Review* ("Immediate City"); and to the editors of the following anthologies—*The Nuyorasian Anthology,* ed. Bino A. Realuyo (Asian American Writers' Workshop, 1999); *American Diaspora: Poetry of Displacement,* eds. Virgil Suarez and Ryan G. Van Cleave (University of Iowa Press, 2001); *The Best American Poetry 2003,* series ed. David Lehman, guest ed. Yusef Komunyakaa (Scribner, 2003); *Like Thunder: Poets Respond to Violence in America,* eds. Virgil Suarez and Ryan G. Van Cleave (University of Iowa Press, 2002); *Poems of New York,* eds. Elizabeth Schmidt and Kevin Young (Knopf, 2002); *Staying Alive: Real Poems for Unreal Times,* ed. Neil Astley (Miramax, 2003)—in which some of these poems have previously appeared. The author would also like to thank the National Endowment for the Arts and the MacDowell Colony for their support.

Contents

3

4

for Suzanne

1

Immediate City

Tall and plural and parallel,
their buff, excited skins
of glass pressed to glass and steel
bronzed by the falling sun,
the city's figmentary buildings dream
that they are one with the One.
Ignoring the office workers
trapped inside their neural nets,
they orient their ecstasy
up past the circling jumbo jets.
Older than the rocks is she

across whom their shadows float.
A million rivers navigate
the necklace at her throat.
The light that falls and falls
shatters in her million prisms.
In one of her million cubicles,
a man tunes his inner mechanisms,
types an endless memorandum.
Time moves slowly, then not at all.
A boy and two girls are
trading secrets down the hall.

Visiting Russia

Another feast day, and the bells are ringing.
The bells are ringing, and not more
than a handful of versts from here,
in the garden of dead hypotheses,
Russia is rising from beds
lavish with nettles and pokeweed,
and from the stalks of fennel obscuring
the mildewed statuary.
Not more than a handful of versts from here,
closer than we thought was possible,
the Tartar ponies are pawing at their stakes,
the tents of the Golden Horde
are stretching from here to there.
Closer than we thought was possible,
Basil, Yaroslavl, the Pantokrator,
the fifth of fifty five-year plans,
the Vladimir Mother of God.
Much has happened in the years between
1200 AD and today, and it is
happening again right now.
To lighten the sleigh, a young girl
is being thrown to the wolves.
The Metropolitan is telling the Old Believers
that only with beauty can we coax
the divine into our nets.
The bones of the young girl thrown to the wolves
are half immersed in strong moonlight.
Thunder in the faraway altitudes,
vacant and subliminal,
is throwing off the rhythms

of the villagers sheaving the rye.
By the year 1200 AD,
Joseph is little more than a memory,
although threads from his coat of many colors,
along with splinters from the True Cross,
the icon, the censer, the axe, are being carried
to the taiga, the tundra, the Baltic,
flat today as a sheet of steel. A sheet of steel
incised to the horizon with faint,
steel-brushed semicircles.
A five-year plan for steel.
A region estimated to be the size
of Australia, untouched by man, rich
with fish and timber and tigers,
iron ore, bauxite, gold, uranium.
At no further cost to themselves,
Peter's cartographers have been given
the pick of the earth. The Caspian Sea,
the Aral Sea, the Sea of Okhotsk.
Few rivers traverse the steppe, its soil
is rocky and meagre, its apprehensive
inhabitants are prey
to princes, chief clerks, marauders,
Kazaks, and holy men. The feet
of their children are bleeding. Pushkin
is standing on a chair in his study.
He has just finished another stanza,
polyhedral and perfectly joined.
His thoughts stray to his faithless wife,
Natalia, née Goncharova. "Nevertheless,"

he says to the walls, "you're one hell of a guy,
Pushkin." Another feast day,
and in the rye field nearest the larger dining room,
where a beautiful, archaic French
is being spoken, where
the candles have been lighted
and the table furnished with soup and bread,
a very old man is sleeping it off—
Sasha, without a tooth in his head.
When Stalin's daughter,
when Stalin's daughter
fled to Delhi, he was still there,
still dreaming of fire and sword,
rebellion and death.

Inventory

The pain in the clavicle. Check. The tendon
throbbing and separating. Check.
The auto-da-fé deep in the heel,

estranging the body from inside the body. Check.
The pressure rises. The lighted fuse

sizzles up the tree of nerves
and explodes in poppy blossoms,
blue blossoms of the anguished cornflower—

the body's aching pyramid
star-ypointed or dotted by
the sleepless eye. Only
the thinnest of scalpels for the transverse incision

by which will be peeled back, one after the other,
the blackening integuments, to expose
what has been waiting underneath:
"Pain (audible at noon)."

Once, in the mountains, to get away from its inflammations,
I stepped over a fieldstone fence
and walked out into a field open to the galaxy
and fell in a ditch. Ouch!

I messed up my leg something fierce.
The experience has been with me ever since.
Check. The cinder in the eye that can't be blinked out.

Interview

That was a pretty roundabout answer to what
I would have to say
was one of the more straightforward of my questions.
But to come back to this thing
you call your near-death experience.
In the accounts I've read, whose credibility,
or lack thereof,
we've already talked about—
that is, their lack thereof—
you say you saw the universe from the outside in, as,
you say, a dense web
of capillaries through which pulsed
corpuscles of light.
(A nice touch, those corpuscles.)
Guy wires, infinite in extension,
were holding down your will,
but—surprise! surprise!—you still had a will
and a body, too.
How can I breathe, without air? you asked yourself.
(I'm wondering about that, too.)
You also say . . . well, you say a lot of things, don't you . . .
You say and say and say.
When the paramedics revive you,
you say, *OK,*
so I'm not God. But neither is God.
To the literally thronging media in the hospital press room,
some of them famous themselves and so
not to be sneezed at,
with a relieved, grateful nation literally hanging
on your every word, you say,

I wish I could shimmy
like my sister Kate.
She shimmies like jelly
on a plate.
Well, I mean, really . . .
excuse me for living, but . . .
and it makes a difference, makes a world of difference . . .
Also, I happened to talk, while preparing
for this broadcast, to your ex, and she said,
and I quote,
Bastard. He could never get enough.
And that cameraman you slugged
outside the Royal Sheraton on your worldwide, and quite lucrative,
lecture tour? He's
a family man and a friend of mine,
and a nicer guy you couldn't hope to meet.

Witch Elegy

Over at the battlements of this misshapen edifice,
    part skyscraper and part ziggurat, I can hear them singing,
"Ding dong, the witch is dead." They're dancing
    the dances they danced before she got here from
who knows where, and feeding a two-story bonfire
    with her inflammable detergents and salves, her furs
skinned from extinct, mythical, and unheard-of animals,
    her ivory-inlaid teak credenzas and chiffoniers.
Messengers from each of the outermost districts
    report that people everywhere are rejoicing,
and in the huts and woodcutters' hovels and
    manor houses the precious relics she hated so much
are being taken from their hiding places and caressed.
    So I guess she must really be dead, the witch,
the poor dead witch, her wings are folded now,
    and her body cognizes, as bodies are forced to,
the dark interstitial liquids of our mortal life.
    "Pity the witch," my heart whispers, "even though
you suffered almost more than the rest."
    And I do pity her. Only now can I see how much
I liked her, even loved her, a little, toward the end,
    when she couldn't stave off the premonition that
she'd soon be a puddle. How often, late in my rounds,
    while barring the hundreds of windows against
the prognosticated sun, I lingered at her half-open door
    and watched while she picked her way through
the Posterior Analytics or the Almagest. She knew
    I was there. She tolerated me. Was it my imagination,
or did she learn to require my presence? Lonely, I thought,
    lonely. Though once I crept in just a little too far,

and she gave me such a look that I staggered away,
    shuddering with visions—a mound of skulls, a
necklace of skulls, skulls on pikestaffs, and other things
    too horrible to put into words, but also, recurring, intercut
with the rest, an image of sunlight on water, which
    a famous poet has written is the very picture
of Paradise. Two things about the witch no one appreciated:
    first, she was beautiful, the very opposite of her own
representation; second, she was the mistress of Time.
    She saw it the way we see the landscape, rolling
or broken, with woods or fields, until it reaches
    a town, complete with slums and palaces. Time
was the wind that blew in her hair, toward Time
    all her researches tended, and from its weeds
she pressed the elixirs that keep those of us
    closest to her as young as we are now—though
it's true that often we're inexplicably tired.

Wolf Soup

In the version of the Three Little Pigs
that I've been given to read my child,
the first two pigs, after the wolf has blown
their houses down
("Little piggy, little piggy, let me come in"),
find refuge with their perspicacious brother.
The wolf, for his part, displays no motivation,
only an impulse arrested
from his body's churning electrolytes
to demolish architectural follies.
He doesn't chase and corner the pigs.
He doesn't have a grudge against the race of pigs,
nor is he in the mood
for pig's knuckles or a nice pig's-ear taco
or even a simple ham sandwich.
And when he comes down the chimney
of the third pig's house—the one he can't
blow down, the one made of brick,
with its dormer windows
tricked out in blue, their trim
decorated with orange daisies—
he suffers for his motiveless malignancy,
in the soup pot waiting for him,
the lid of which has been removed with a
timely flourish, nothing worse than a scalding,
and runs back to his lair
somewhere over the hill.
Everyone has survived their lessons.
Everyone, as in the Last Judgment of the Zoroastrians,
is saved, even the wolf,

today exterminated
across much of the world, and almost so
in the forty-eight contiguous states.
The real story, which is locked in my desk
while I write this encryption, goes,
as you all remember, differently.
In it, the wolf eats the first two pigs,
but the third pig, the smart pig,
the shrewd, shrewd little pig, eats him in a soup
flavored with the turnips gathered
in a memorable prior episode.
Long did that pig rest a pensive trotter on the windowsill,
as he looked down the dusty road
travelled by the wolf.
His brothers were dead, his mother
unapproachable in her grief, and for weeks
the taste of wolf, at once unguent, farinaceous, brittle, and serene,
touched his mind with a golden fire.
In a pig's eye, he thought,
as his molecules began to recombine . . .
My son might be ready for this version of the story.
Like most four-year-olds,
he's precocious and realistic and bloody-minded.
He already knows, for example, that Jack
was nothing better than a common thief,
and has at some point observed
that giants let their fingernails grow,
sometimes to hideous lengths.

Very Simple and Like a Song

That furrow in the hill once must have been
a notch in a sheer cliff.
The land is all changed around here,
due to the work of wind and water,
but not so much that we can't think back
to what it must have been:
on the plateau beyond what must have been the cliff,
endless animal herds mollified in the sun,
kneeling and browsing,
and the lazy embankments descending to the watercourse
strewn with a little yellow flower, now extinct,
which must have resembled the celandine.
We talk in the presumptive,
but we know we can declare this much:
they were afraid,
so they climbed down the notch to this place,
more protected by far then than now.
What were they afraid of? Not
the animals but the fact of the animals,
that the animals existed,
that they themselves existed,
that everything existed when it might as well not have—
which was their one and only revelation,
which they would come back to again and again
down the hundred and fifty thousand years
and never get more than an inch farther with it than they were now,
when all they felt was terror.
So they climbed down here and hid.
And, then, they taught themselves to bury their dead.
They felt the pressure of the nothingness around them,

and at this place they began the digging of graves,
with their flaked hand axes.
One so took to the pressure and the feeling of it
he would teach himself to manufacture
surplus dead to feed the graves.
One female taught herself to whisper.
They would someday become
Euripides, Heloise, Saladin,
Swedenborg, Nell Gywnn, Mencius,
Gandhi and Mandela,
the Pankhursts, Captain Beefheart, Dr. Dre,
and one Terry Butler,
who shook Joe Turner's hand
in a bar in Kansas City,
and shook the hand of Rahsaan Roland Kirk.
All the while, the fear
lived right beside them,
and the sound effects accompanying it were drums drumming,
so insistent, and so convenient that they
convinced themselves that everything was fine
as long as the drums were drumming,
that only when the drums stopped would they be required to worry.

Lecture

Moving on to the next slide,
we can see, twisted and deliberately coarsened as it is,
the exact same theme,
revisited now with an
ambition and gigantism made all the more monstrous
by the still soaring line,
instinct with delicacy and intelligence,
by the palette still fresh and strange,
the siennas and umbers
and crimsons and yellows seasoned
with the crushed carapaces of iridescent damselflies.
The silence, as in a sacristy,
with little rustlings and breathings,
is still invested in subsidiary forms and minor passages of paint.
The anatomical tenderness is apparent still in the rendering of
the sexual *disjecta membra,*
which serve at the same time
both the impulse to drama and the need for structure.
Made he them male and female.
Made he them done and then undone,
only to be resurrected
(the word is not too strong)
divorced from the bodies appended to which
they once possessed function, integrity, reality.
How we long, when we
observe these vulval forms
drawn with an insane precision,
these preputial folds, these tubes and columns and placental blocks,
for the old nudes.
Where I have placed my cursor,

note the black markings—defining almost the face we know
from the thousand self-portraits—
on this amorphous blob,
this howl of paint the color of flayed skin.
They are the last remnants of this same self, the splendid subjectivity
that gave such excitement to
his Magenta period, his Geometric period,
his Whatever-I-Say-Is-Art-Is-Art
period, his several neoclassical periods, his war
period, his Babylonian,
Egyptian, and Chinese periods,
his Long-Years-In-The-Asylum period.
How strange to see him now,
as bewildered as we are,
crouched and terrified
in a petty corner of his canvas,
as his great spaces collapse inward.
Before we turn away in shock and horror, though,
we shouldn't fail to acknowledge again
that at one time
when he would pick up a stick to draw
the birds stopped their singing and waited in anticipation,
when he drew an arabesque
in the sand, the earth itself
shivered with delight.

North of Manhattan

You can take the Dyre Avenue bus to where the subway terminates
just inside the Bronx
and be downtown before you realize
how quickly your body has escaped your mind,
stretching down the tracks on a beam
until the band snaps and the body slips free and is gone,
out the crashing doors, through the stiles,
and up the long chutes,
to burn both ways at once down the avenues,
ecstatic in its finitude,
with all the other bodies,
the bundles of molecules
fusing and dispersing on the sidewalks.
Ten to the hundredth power,
bundles of molecules are looking at paintings,
bundles of molecules are eating corn muffins,
crabcakes, shad roe, spring lamb, rice pudding.
Bundles of molecules are talking to each other,
sotto voce or in a commanding voice—
"I agree with you one hundred percent, Dog";
"I looked for you today, but you'd already gone";
"I've left the Amended Restated Sublease Agreement on your desk";
"I'm going home now,
and you think about what you did."
The ear grows accustomed to wider and wider intervals.
The eye senses shapes in the periphery
toward which it dares not turn to look.
One bundle is selling another a playback machine,
a six-square-inch wax-paper reticule
of powdered white rhinoceros horn,

an off-season-discounted ticket to Machu Picchu,
a gas-powered generator
for when the lights go out,
a dime bag of Mexican brown.
It is four o'clock in the afternoon.
The sunlight is stealing inch by inch
down the newly repointed redbrick wall.
She comes into the kitchen wrapped in the quilt
and watches as he fries eggs.
"After what just happened, you want to eat?" she says in disgust.
Will she or will she not, back in the bedroom,
lift the gun from the holster
and put it in her purse? The mind, meanwhile,
is still somewhere around Tremont Avenue,
panting down the tracks, straining
from the past to the vanishing present.
It will never catch up
and touch the moment. It will always be
in this tunnel of its forever,
where aquamarine crusted bulbs feed on a darkness
that looks all around without seeing,
and fungus, earlike, starved for light, sprouts
from walls where drops of rusted water
condense and drip.

Don't say I didn't warn you about this.
Don't say my concern for your welfare
never extended to my sharing the terrible and addictive secrets
that only death can undo.
Because I'm telling you now

that you can also take the same bus north,
crossing over against the traffic spilling out of the mall
and waiting twenty minutes in the kiosk with the Drambuie ad.
There. Isn't that better?
More passengers are getting off than on.
The girl with the skates going home from practice
will soon get off, as will
the old woman whose license to drive has been taken from her.
They will enter houses with little gazebos tucked in their gardens.
And then, for just a while, the mind will disembark from the body,
relaxed on its contoured plastic seat,
and go out to make fresh tracks in the snow
and stand and breathe under the imaginary trees—
the horsehair pine, the ambergris tree,
the tree that the bulbul loves,
the nebula tree . . .

2

North

As if in a well a thousand dead cities deep,
all over the hemisphere
the people sleep—
their mysteries still unsolved,

their doors shut tight.
Inside, a voice croons
Be mine tonight
to their deaf selves,

deafer than the stars.
A cold front floods
down the isobars
and inches up the pipes,

silent but in motion,
inching as steadily
as an ocean
to float them through the silence,

the cold, appetizing silence,
and wash them up on a shore
of ice far to the north,
farther north than Labrador.

Fractured Fairytale

"You're coming up daisies, moose and squirrel,"
that same red-eyed, locked-and-loaded figure
intones in ten-second intervals—
blood grinning in his beard,
his finger squeezing the trigger . . .

But, gosh, Bullwinkle, isn't that guy the eternal recurrence of the same
reductive nemesis in whose name
the generalized life pulverizes
our beautiful particularities,
the horn of the moose and the tooth of the squirrel.
What's it all about, anyway?

"I don't know, Rock.
I don't even know that I don't know.
But if I had my druthers,
I'd just curl up by the fire with my books
—my books!—
'cause they burn so nice and slow."

Superman Agonistes

"When my X-ray eyes look through the humans
to the need inside,
glowing red and green,
my blood cells collide,

my lungs collapse,
my cortex rebels,
and my heart wraps
a bomb around itself

and threatens to kill us both.
But I can't stay away.
I have to fly down
to watch them pray,

to watch them couple,
to watch them fight,
exposing myself
to their kryptonite."

Aphasia

His signs flick off.
His names of birds
and his beautiful words—
eleemosynary, fir, cinerarium, reckless—
skip like pearls from a snapped necklace
scattering over linoleum.

His thinking won't
venture out of his mouth.
His grammar heads south.
Pathetic his subjunctives; just as pathetic
his mangling the emphatic enclitic
he once was the master of.

Still, all in all, he has
his inner weather of pure meaning,
though the wind is keening
through his Alps and his clouds hang low
and the forecast is "Rain mixed with snow,
heavy at times."

The Scholar

Illusions she didn't know she had were shattered when
she saw in the text she was cleaning up—
the corrupt recension of the now lost text—
not the cypress of heaven
or the morphology of a recurring type
or the riverbank where a god dances
but her own self's circumstances,

and not in the lover but the miserable sinner
who, as the poem trembled
to the death of its god,
drew back in fear
and so came to be noticed
by the demon who so resembled
her sworn enemy in her department,
with his bleak chin and his knowing look.
Though prodded by him she did write the book

that captured it all—god, demon, lover, avatar,
the ascension by night, the great battle,
the sobbing behind the ruined lattice—
and suspended it between her mother tongues
in the cat's cradle of her scholarly apparatus—
made from shards, really, but mysteriously there.

Anima

Not Garbo, for instance, or my wife but white, though flecks
and patches of melanin coruscate
the olive acres rising between
her breasts and her thighs,
and African ovals frame her eyes.
Twenty-eight and chemically complex,

she studies all night for her GED.
At dawn, she goes out to do
what her doctor tells her to do:
dig in her garden, where she grows
the rose they call the cabbage rose
and the huge iris they call the fleur-de-lis.

But every so often her mind goes slack
and desperate. Spectral and pale,
she walks her hills in a long black veil
mourning me—her quizzical, her other,
her bitter, prodigal, absconded half.
Where, just where, am I that I can never come back?

Thelma

We have a small place on an ugly street,
though we keep it spick and span.
I take the garbage out, but you,
Thelma, you the man—

brilliant as the velvet eye
setting off a peacock's feather,
rayed as the sun is rayed
through storming, broken weather

and gilt-edged clouds. And me?
I strip to my birthday suit
and scream out the window at the Yemeni kids,
who scream back, *"Sharmout!"*

rolling by on their Rollerblades.
You and me, Thelma, and the little squirt,
with me on the stoop
in my cap turned backward and my undershirt.

Tree

for Richard Wilbur

Three streets south of where I sit
is a city park with a plane tree in it.

From any place you choose to enter,
the tree forms the park's pole and perfect center.

Its slight, heliotropic, side-
wise bias, its height, and its wide,

rustling canopy all testify that it has won
its long negotiations with the sun,

and now simply distributes the breeze,
and keeps guard over these

ruminant people who stand before
the local memorial to the war

or sit on the benches ordering the mess
and stilling the noise of consciousness,

while the tree arches above them, serene,
mottled, magnificent, Platonic, and green.

Ailanthus

In their distorting internal mirrors,
the battered and in pain
become the dragons mauling them.
Their spirits drain

to their spleens, which manufacture
a substance, viscous, green,
that catalyzes their hearts'
colorless acetylene,

igniting their dragon breath.
Then they breathe and burn.
The ones who did them dirt
are done to a turn.

The ones who stopped to watch
are torched to black pathetic stems
by holographic Greek fire
and ICBMs.

And what happens to
those servants of the state
whose fault it all is is too
painful to relate.

Brothers and sisters to dragons!—
but only in their dreams
the mountain spews,
the fissure steams.

Elsewhere, the tree-of-heaven grows—
in deserted parking lots,
auto graveyards, abandoned
garden plots.

The wind in its leaves
is dry, arrhythmic, and sad.
Everyone, it whispers, has their reasons,
a few of which are bad.

Survivor

We hold it against you that you survived.
People better than you are dead,
but you still punch the clock.
Your body has wizened but has not bled

its substance out on the killing floor
or flatlined in intensive care
or vanished after school
or stepped off the ledge in despair.

Of all those you started with,
only you are still around;
only you have not been listed with
the defeated and the drowned.

So how could you ever win our respect?—
you, who had the sense to duck,
you, with your strength almost intact
and all your good luck.

The Day of the Sun

Arriving early at the limit of understanding,
I managed to find a good seat,
and settled in with the others,
who were fanning away the heat

with their programs full of blank pages.
The orchestra was in place,
and soon the show started.
First, deep space

rose high and flooded the stage,
immersing all the spots
where our thoughts could have fixed
if our minds had thoughts.

Which they didn't. Then
the sun came out and stood.
That was all that happened,
and ever would.

3

The Nature of the Chemical Bond

1

On our drives into the northern and central reaches of the Confederacy, my father—a scrupulous person, slow, deliberate, rule-bound, reflective, melancholy, orderly (and all of this from birth)—would suddenly become adventurous. If there was a way to get to where we were going that was innovative or idiosyncratic or held out the promise of drama, or just gave him a chance to improvise and navigate that the road suggested by common sense and the Triple-A map didn't offer, he'd be on it in a flash. When he heard—and he always heard—the words "back roads" in his head, his inborn caution vanished. Visions of horse farms and weathered barns with Mail Pouch chewing-tobacco signs stencilled and fading on their sides and big woods with little hollows where the people lived a life that had gone on long enough to look as if it had gone on forever clouded his brain and turned him away from his dharma-ridden self. In his crisp, musical Bangalore accent, he would say "Let us take the back roads" at some point in our trips, even though this was when the interstate-highway system was still an unelaborated sketch on the landscape, so, apart from the occasional few hours on a turnpike, most of the roads leading to our largely rural destinations could safely be called back roads. My mother eyed him with exasperation, but, in those days, when she was young and hadn't freed herself completely from inherited imperatives of wifely deference and was, besides, still daunted enough by America to keep her natural rebelliousness to herself, she usually gave in. I was in the backseat with my sister (a toddler, oblivious, often carsick), nursing a flourishing skepticism about my parents' ability to negotiate the New World. I thought we'd get lost, and we did 50 percent of the time, because the roads that looked straightforward on the map would turn out to have uncanny forks and folds and confusing crossroads. We would find ourselves on one or another of those wrong forks and have to heave the car around or drive on, sometimes for miles and miles, until we came across a gas station or a store, where my father, embarrassed but still game, would ask for directions. If the people we were petitioning to set us straight were amazed or affronted by the sudden appearance in Arcadia of a family of East Indians—something unthinkable in those years—they didn't let on. Polite and prolix, they told us carefully what to do; and once, in Virginia, on a hot August day, when I was nine, a white-haired, wet-eyed old man gave me a cold eight-ounce bottle of Coca-Cola (I can still taste it) and took me out to the back of his antique store to show me a duck pond he had built—with, he said, his "own two hands"—which had a miniature artificial grotto and a miniature blue-washed waterwheel being turned by an artificial waterfall.

Where were we going while we were getting lost on those long drives? We were going to Civil War battlefields. We were on our way to Manassas and Antietam and Chancellorsville; to Harper's Ferry, the MacLean house, Petersburg, and the Wilderness. We were rolling through the monotonous, low-lying country between the Alleghenies and the Blue Ridge to Gettysburg, which we stopped at five times in the early and mid-sixties. We were pointing the nose of our 1960 two-tone coppertone Chevy three-speed station wagon—three-on-the-tree the transmission was nicknamed, because the gearshift was built into the steering column—in the direction of Vicksburg; though, to my father's bitter regret, we never quite made it to that sleepy river town, crucial to the canvas of the war he was painting in his head because its investiture and seizure by Grant in the summer of 1863—exactly a hundred and one years before we approached its vicinity—secured the length of the Mississippi for the Union and brought the defeat of the Confederacy almost to inevitability. We didn't get any farther than Shiloh on that trip, Shiloh of terrible memory. Whose memory, though? That is a question my father didn't, and still doesn't, ask, a question which, when lifted up and turned over in his mind, is found to be crawling on its underside with the things designed to excite his intellectual disgust—metaphysics, cultural, racial, and national identity, psychology, historicity. "It was interesting," he will say when I ask him what on earth he had been thinking. When pressed, he will counterattack and throw the burden of those vacant and interminable drives—with my mother mystified in the front and my sister carsick in the rear—back on me. "We wanted you to learn American history"—though we never went to Faneuil Hall or Plymouth Rock or the Liberty Bell or Valley Forge or Colonial Williamsburg or Monticello or Fort Ticonderoga or Fallen Timbers or the Great Snake Mound, which is not far from Columbus, Ohio, where we were living through those years. And our explorations of Washington, D.C., hard by a lot of the battlefields we visited, were perfunctory, and mostly involved Ford's Theatre, Mrs. Greenhow, and the Lincoln Memorial.

It was always the War between the States for my father. Dred Scott. Stoneman's cavalry. Mosby's rangers. Bloody Kansas. The affair of the *Trent.* The *Monitor* versus the *Merrimac.* He read and re-read Carl Sandburg's biography of Lincoln and *A Stillness at Appomattox* and *Andersonville. The American Heritage Picture History of the Civil War,* with its beautiful reproductions of chromolithographs and Winslow Homer oils, was a fixture on his night table. He collected battlefield brochures by the dozen. He knew the odd facts: Miss Laura Keene starred in *Our American Cousin* on Lincoln's fatal night; the Empress Carlota lived on, demented in Paris, until 1927. He knew the even facts, the awful facts: six hundred and twenty thousand dead in carnage up to that time never inflicted on humankind. He rehearsed the great battlefield eloquences: *It is well that war is so terrible—we should grow too fond of it; We cannot dedicate, we cannot consecrate, we cannot hallow this ground.* By day, he was a physical chemist. By night, he was bivouacked with the Army of the Potomac. By day, he investigated the nature of the chemical bond—the three-electron bond; the partial ionic character of covalent bonds between unlike atoms; the hybridization of bond orbitals; hyperconjugation and fractional bonding in metals; clouds of electron probabilities along that mysterious border where the atomic and the molecular realms interpenetrate, where matter becomes number and number matter, revealed to him by infrared and nuclear-magnetic-resonance spectroscopy, electron-spin-resonance spectroscopy, absorption and emission spectra. Instruments other than the human eye have articulated the properties of light: it has a dual character, wave and quanta; it has different wavelengths. Newton, Herschel, Ritter, Young, Fraunhofer, Kirchhoff, Bunsen, Angstrom, Michelson, Bohr, Benoit, Fabry, Perot, Coblentz, and Raman are some of the names by which the minds that have discovered these astonishing things are known. There exists light of wavelengths longer and shorter than the wavelengths of visible light. From discrete bands on either side of the tiny band of the electromagnetic spectrum that makes an impression on our retinas, light directed onto a sample compound of given thickness will make the atomic particles glow or will be swallowed up and leave a shadow. The glowing or the shadow (these are, of course, just metaphors) can be captured by spectroscopes (from the Latin for *appearance*, from the Greek for *to see*), in the form of spectra. These spectra my father brought home to work on at the kitchen table. In his firm, elegant script, he covered the graph paper on which they were captured in inky lines with his mathematical runes.

When he took a break, he turned to the Great Rebellion. A socialist of the mild, Fabian, Congress Party variety—Nehru and the vegetarian George Bernard Shaw were among our household gods—he might, if asked, have described the war as a socialist war, prosecuted, whatever the concomitant or efficient reasons, to eliminate capitalism's most vicious practice, chattel slavery. No one was around to ask him, though, except me, and I couldn't have framed such a question. So he was required to confess nothing. I can't remember his ever telling me anything about the Civil War that carried the faintest odor of morality or politics or interpretation. He seemed to accept unquestioningly the then (and still) prevalent notion of the war by which the imperatives of the North were balanced by the valor and passion and superior skillfulness of the underdog South, lifting the conflict beyond partisanship, beyond good and evil, clarifying it until it became a smooth, simple drama whose meaning was contained deep within itself. He fell in step with the thinking about the war that saw motives as local, and the deeper causalities subsumed by tactics, strategy, movement, battle lines, salients and bridgeheads, preponderant forces and materiel, clemencies and inclemencies of weather, and chaotic mischances and coincidences. In the books he read, in the brochures he collected, there was no interest in justification, no question of right or wrong. Everybody was forgiven in the end, except that small gallery of characters that includes Vallandigham, Quantrill, and John Wilkes Booth. This was perfect for him. It gave scope to his instinctive empiricism and his discomfort with generalities, which were suspicious with hidden and untenable assumptions. The Civil War was as fundamental, as immutable, as the submolecular realm, a modernist war made for the modernist he was then, and still is, as clear and impenetrable as a line by Wallace Stevens or a Calder mobile. It referred to nothing but itself. Wrapped in its structures, though, was a human heroism pure and appalling and desperate, so pure and appalling and desperate that it, too, seems immutable. This was something my father understood. These were the desperate frequencies that set his atomic particles vibrating. He had been orphaned of his father at an early age in a cholera epidemic that almost took him away at the same time (he'd also survived smallpox). His family had been thrown into poverty and a humiliating dependency. They hadn't experienced the most terrible Indian destitution, but India has many destitutions, and they always heard one or another coughing and shuffling outside their door. His education had been financed entirely by the scholarships and fellowships available in what was then the princely state of Mysore—which may have been the most advanced of the Indian princely states in the decades before Independence—and in the world beyond. If the massive silence that lies at the center of his psyche is any indication, his character had not only been defined but pretty much exhausted by frugality, anxiety, and constant labor. His one chance—his one grace—had been science. He once said to me, in wonder rather than bitterness, "If I hadn't found science, I would have been nothing."

Hundreds of thousands of men throwing themselves against the merciless fire of a technology that had left the tactics of their officers far behind. The desperation. "Fundamental and astounding," Lincoln called it, meaning that even he had no words. The self moves beyond dread and terror and confronts its essential poverty and nakedness and isolation. This my father understood, too well and too immediately. The conflict was vivid to his moody, wordless fatalism, his sense, so strange in the bountiful Middle America of the early sixties, that all choices narrowed to one choice, which wasn't a choice at all but was construed as such by our incorrigible gift for deceiving ourselves into thinking we're free. And so, the following, suitably edited to disguise their violence, became the bedside anecdotes of my childhood's middle years: in the twilight of early May, a mistaken fusillade from his own men cuts down Stonewall Jackson, out scouting the enemy lines (Lee, my father says, will miss him at Gettysburg); the citizens of Cherbourg come down to the quays to watch the *Alabama* and the *Kearsarge* trading broadsides in the harbor (eventually, my father says, the captain of the *Alabama* will strike his colors and then throw himself overboard); Forrest's cavalry harasses the flanks, exploding out of the woods and forcing the Union soldiers to scatter across the deadfall and the scrub; in one half hour, after a blundering delay by his generals, Grant loses seven thousand men, dead or maimed. These stories had no interest for me when I was a kid. Their ontology was all wrong. Their being was continuous with the being around me. They took place in a terrain undifferentiated from the terrain we inhabited. The fields and woods were the same fields and woods we saw and knew, except for the fact that they were in Virginia or Tennessee. We knew people in Columbus whose great-grandfathers had been Union soldiers, which excited my father but, secretly, depressed me because of its quotidian lack of access to the different geographies where conflict and war, I thought, quite reasonably, should occur, places like the ones in the movies I loved—Ardennes (*Battleground*), medieval England (*The Adventures of Robin Hood*), or full fathom five in the Pacific Ocean (*Run Silent, Run Deep*). When my father walked me over battlefields, instructing me about unwavering lines and salients, I felt as heavy as mercury, inert, bored, baffled, as baffled as I was when, years before I had the requisite mathematical knowledge or skill, he sat me down and with excruciating patience explained the concept of a limit and the mysteries, stunning to me now but impossible then, of the fundamental theorem of calculus. I did, though, understand something in those excursions. I took something away. Something came along, prodigious as a revelation. I understood him, my father. I developed a precocious awareness of his difference. And I felt guilty about having seen him as he really was. I understood something about him that a son should probably not understand about a father, at least not at that age. The passage to America had, happily for him, thrown him free, but it had also stripped him down to his naked soul. Almost to this day, like the sons of Noah, I have longed to walk backward and cover up the nakedness, the drunkenness of his intellectual obsessions, his naked, unheard-of obsessions, irritably reaching after fact and reason to fold him back into motives less uncanny and more reminiscent. Occasionally in recent years, I have engaged him in the game of Twenty Questions with which he tends to deflect assaults on his privacy.

"Was it America, Dad? Was it because you liked America?"

"No. It wasn't America."

"Was Lincoln like Gandhi? They were both assassinated, right?"

"No. Gandhi was religious."

"Was slavery like Untouchability?"

"That was India. This is America."

"Did it remind you of the war in the Mahabharata? That was a fratricidal war."

"The Mahabharata is just a story."

2

My parents didn't go on vacations when they were young in India before and after the Second World War. India hadn't yet experienced the benefits of industrialization. Time wasn't broken up into units that represented work and leisure. Rest for the body and the soul was found in the many religious festivals that dot the Indian lunar calendar, and that bear the stamp of a cyclical rural life and an ancient nature-worshipping religion: Sankranthi, in January, the rice-crop festival; Shivarathri, in February, when the males of Shaivite families fast all night in the temple, and Shiva, creator and destroyer, the embodiment in the Indian imagination of time itself, brushes against their inner life; Ugadi, in March, the new-year festival, which my mother's feast-loving family—like my father's from a Tamil-speaking community in Bangalore, a Kannada-speaking city, where the new year falls on a different day than in Tamil Nadu—would celebrate not once but twice; Ramanavami, in June, the birthday of Rama, famous in South India for its day- and nightlong music concerts; the birthday of Krishna in August, Gokulashtami, a long fast followed by a feast at midnight on the appointed day, the moment of Krishna's birth; Ganapathi, in early October, the festival of Ganesh—fat, affectionate, elephant-headed god who eases the passage from life to death; and, finally, in late October and early November, the dates determined by the phases of the moon, the two great harvest festivals— Navarathri, when for nine nights the *grahas,* the elements that make human life possible, among them earth, water, fire, the implements of the field, and the benisons of the cow, are given a grateful devotion; and Depavali, the festival of lights, dear to my mother's heart because when she was a girl her father, who was the chief engineer for Mysore state, would every year be invited with his family to the festivities at the rococo palace of the Wodeyar Maharajah of Mysore.

The closest my father ever got to the rococo palace of the Wodeyar Maharajah of Mysore was a brother-in-law of his who for a while owned a small bakery that sometimes supplied the royals with bread. This brother-in-law, the only source of income in my father's family after the death of my grandfather, decided one day to run off to Bombay with a young girl of his acquaintance, forcing my father's sister to move back to my grandmother's crowded, anxious household. When my mother rhapsodizes about the feast of Depavali at the palace, with its army of cooks, its opulent service, its spectacular illuminations and fireworks—or when she describes the great yearly *darbar* where her father, dressed, along with the other servants of the crown, in a black silk waistcoat and a turban, offered his prince a silver rupee as a token of his fealty, and was subsequently reëndowed with the same coin by that generous, farsighted sovereign—my father can be counted on for a snort of derision. He is partial, though, to South Indian vegetarian cooking, and, like all people who have been truly poor, thinks of food as the ultimate wealth. So he fell in with my mother's desire to re-create at least some of the feasts of her youth. In those years, the only store in America that sold authentic Indian groceries was Kalustyan's, on Lexington Avenue, in Manhattan. From 1961 to 1968, we drove to New York every summer to shop there, staying with a physicist friend of our family who worked at Brookhaven National Laboratory, on Long Island. With the Chevy loaded down with supplies for a year—hundred-pound burlap sacks of rice, ten-pound bags of every kind of lentil and pulse, little vials of precious Kashmiri saffron, ginger roots in the dozens, crystals of camphor, tens of thousands of black mustard seeds, chilies, fresh and dried, fresh and dried coconut, coriander, seed and plant, peppercorns, rock candy, dried curry leaves, cardamom, fenugreek, asafetida, Japanese eggplants, and Chinese melons—we would drive back to Ohio. On the Pennsylvania Turnpike that first time, my father saw a sign pointing to Gettysburg. He decided to turn off and take a look, and liked what he saw. This was what set him off, the Aristotelian efficient cause. On each trip to New York after that, until my mother put a stop to it, we would visit the battlefield. During one trip, we went to Gettysburg twice, on the way east and again on the way back west because he had seen in a bookstore in Manhattan a photograph of a Confederate sniper's nest built from rocks and wanted to find out if it had been preserved.

"We have been here already," my mother said. "We have been here ten days ago."

3

We were strange. We were doubly strange: strange because Indians are strange even in India, having been exiled from time and history by an overdeveloped, supersaturated civilization, and strange also because no one remotely resembling us had ever before lived where we lived. But I was the only person in my family beset and burdened by this strangeness. My parents were absorbed in the details of our material and spiritual survival—my mother, gregarious and active, was busy with her intense domestic arrangements; my father was either working on his spectra or off with the Army of the Potomac. I, though, was transfixed by our image reflected in the order that surrounded us. As painful as it was to look, I couldn't in those days tear myself away; and I became trapped by what I saw us as in the mirror of our benign, distant, Protestant Midwestern world. I was like Shakespeare's liquid prisoner pent in walls of glass, and eventually had to ooze my way free through the cracks formed in that glass by the earthquakes of the 1960s. This confused us as a family, forced us to expend psychic resources we had always carefully husbanded, and made us all unhappy, especially my father, who had wanted me to climb up, climb up to his impossible level of concretion and discipline. I didn't come back to the Civil War for a long time. But then, slowly, peculiarly compelled, I did, watching the documentaries on public television and browsing in the history shelves of libraries and bookstores. I kept this resurrected interest secret from my father for years. One Thanksgiving in the mid-1990s, though, when I thought I was safe, I mentioned that I'd recently read Shelby Foote's account of Gettysburg, and was surprised at how clearly I could visualize the battle, and see it unfold hour by hour. He didn't say much at the time. His response was delayed, and when it came it was calculated and massive. Three weeks later he sent me a Christmas present, a first edition of the two volumes of the *Personal Memoirs of U. S. Grant.* When I called to thank him, I told him that Gertrude Stein had had a high appreciation of the memoirs. He said that was good, and that he might read Stein (he never did). And then, with both of us recognizing that the long interregnum had finally ended, that we were stuck with each other, we got into it about Grant. Grant was fine until he became president, I said, but what a terrible president. The corruption! The railroads! This agitated him. It wasn't Grant's fault, he couldn't be held responsible for his corrupt companions. The Civil War had brought changes that no one could have encompassed, not even Lincoln. Look at how right Grant was about the Mexican War. Look at how he wrote those memoirs while he was dying of cancer, in order to provide for his wife. That alone was enough to wipe away the blemishes of his administration. Grant was always impressive. His only fault was that he was too trusting. Grant, my father said, had requited himself. Grant, my father insisted before we hung up, was an underestimated man.

4

The Disappearances

"Where was it one first heard of the truth?"

On a day like any other day,
like "yesterday or centuries before,"
in a town with the one remembered street,
shaded by the buckeye and the sycamore—
the street long and true as a theorem,
the day like yesterday or the day before,
the street you walked down centuries before—
the story the same as the others flooding in
from the cardinal points is
turning to take a good look at you.
Every creature, intelligent or not, has disappeared—
the humans, phosphorescent,
the duplicating pets, the guppies and spaniels,
the Woolworth's turtle that cost forty-nine cents
(with the soiled price tag half peeled on its shell)—
but, from the look of things, it only just happened.
The wheels of the upside-down tricycle are spinning.
The swings are empty but swinging.
And the shadow is still there, and there
is the object that made it,
riding the proximate atmosphere,
oblong and illustrious above
the dispeopled bedroom community,
venting the memories of those it took,
their corrosive human element.
This is what you have to walk through to escape,
transparent but alive as coal dust.
This is what you have to hack through,
bamboo-tough and thickly clustered.

The myths are somewhere else, but here are the meanings,
and you have to breathe them in
until they burn your throat
and peck at your brain with their intoxicated teeth.
This is you as seen by them, from the corner of an eye
(was that the way you were always seen?).
This is you when the President died
(the day is brilliant and cold).
This is you poking a ground-wasps' nest.
This is you at the doorway, unobserved,
while your aunts and uncles keen over the body.
This is your first river, your first planetarium, your first Popsicle.
The cold and brilliant day in six-color prints—
but the people on the screen are black and white.
Your friend's mother is saying,
Hush, children! Don't you understand history is being made?
You do, and you still do. Made and made again.
This is you as seen by them, and them as seen by you,
and you as seen by you, in five dimensions,
in seven, in three again, then two,
then reduced to a dimensionless point
in a universe where the only constant is the speed of light.
This is you at the speed of light.

Baby Baby

Choices have been made that I had nothing to do with—
mistakes have been made,
and, worse than that,
Death has been served tea and fresh figs.
I was not present in that room,
at the table polished with citron oil.
I did not take part in the extended discussion
whereby the decision was refined.
So don't point a finger at me someday.
I was here by the crib, looking at you
chewing your toes,
blowing raspberries,
blowing little thought balloons
with your labials, fricatives, glottal stops, and retroflexes,
your mint-condition neurons firing.
(The language can't be understood,
but the purpose is plain.)
I was here advising you that even though
all the women want to stroke you
and all the men want to be your pal
you should probably start developing
your own resources.
Popularity like that never lasts.
I was saying how difficult it is to be
courteous, loyal, thrifty,
brave, cheerful, obedient, and wise
separately, let alone all at once.
I was pointing you far into the future, to the day
you go down to the river
and wade out knee-deep in the sacred element

and turn and see on the riverbank
seven luminous beings lined up and looking at you.
To which of them will you put your question
when you wade back? The Christians say
the story of the universe is the story of a boy and his dad.
They are absolutely right.
I can see that now, waiting here
for the smiles I'd kill for,
watching you as you sleep curling your fist,
which in a time I can barely recollect
did not, or maybe did, exist.

The Painted Things

Never as slowly as you do now
have I seen you take the painted things off before.

One hour isn't enough for the bangle on your wrist,
one day for your jewel-encrusted breastplate.
One night dies
expecting your velvet garter.

The glacial tick in the moraine,
the clock of radium in the stone
can't keep the time it takes for your sky blue blouse
to be slipped from your shoulder.

And as for your *sous-vêtements*—
the sun will burn out before
I can put my paws on those,

sleeping on my paws at your little desk
as I wait for you,
because I have eyes slow enough for you,
I have the eyes to wait for you.

A Fable

The boy and the father walked beside the donkey.
The road was gray, and dust rose to its vanishing point;
gray dust choked the leaves of the few
asthmatic cottonwoods along the dry creekbeds.
The sky was hot to the touch.
"Why not ride the donkey, as it's so hot?"
passersby on the road suggested.
The boy and the father whispered to each other.
(They were more like brothers
than they were like son and father.)
The father got up on the donkey.
Other passersby, or maybe the same ones
doubling back—the only leisure-time activity
in that part of the world involved
walking up and down the dusty road—
said, "Selfish, selfish old man! Think of your boy,
whose legs can't bear the insult
of this road, let alone the heat's."
They went on a ways the way they were,
because they didn't want what scrutinized them
with such detachment to think they were slaves
to public opinion. Then they traded places.
A mile later, an old woman on a porch, rocking
and shading her eyes from a sun that seemed
not to dwindle but instead hammered
the sky to a thinness irreconcilable
with the laws of nature, shouted out,
"Worthless! Letting your old father walk!"
So the father climbed up behind the boy,
and they both rode the donkey.

This incited an animal lover,
wearing a hat like the ones you see
in the wood-block prints of the Japanese,
to screaming flights of invective
for burdening the donkey with two bodies. So,
abashed, they got down, and they carried the donkey.
The donkey howled and evacuated in terror,
but they carried him anyway, over the undulating road
and across the boulder-studded arroyos.
They came to a town and lived there for a while,
and then moved to a larger town, and then
to the fabled city, suspended
on a plain between two mountain ranges.
They lived in a room in a house in a suburb
known for its featurelessness,
the two of them, with the donkey.
The father couldn't work anymore—
the business with the donkey had broken him forever—
so the son went out alone in the world.
He was the one who buried the donkey,
in the dead of night, when no one was looking.
Later, he buried his father, too,
but this time in daylight, in a decent graveyard.
He didn't care about his place in the world,
but he married a woman who did, and had children
and prospered, in a manner of speaking.
The tally of the generations begins with him
and extends down the centuries
and across the hemispheres
and numbers CPAs and bookies,

coopers and wheelwrights,
neurologists, embezzlers, claims adjusters,
and linemen for the county.
And, though diverse and ignorant
of one another, though pressed like grapes
through the bewildering human genotypes,
each of them has this one thing in common—
each knows, obscurely, unconsciously,
without knowing how he knows, that
only the complicated, ambiguous victories
are worth having, those that take place
under the sun, above
the boulder-studded arroyo,
with the dust, grayer than bone, rising on the road.

The Long Meadow

Near the end of one of the old poems, the son of righteousness,
the source of virtue and civility,
on whose back the kingdom is carried
as on the back of the tortoise the earth is carried,
passes into the next world.
The wood is dark. The wood is dark,
and on the other side of the wood the sea is shallow, warm, endless.
In and around it, there is no threat of life—
so little is the atmosphere charged with possibility that
he might as well be wading through a flooded basement.
He wades for what seems like forever,
and never stops to rest in the shade of the metal rain trees
springing out of the water at fixed intervals.
Time, though endless, is also short,
so he wades on, until he walks out of the sea and into the mountains,
where he burns on the windward slopes and freezes in the valleys.
After unendurable struggles,
he finally arrives at the celestial realm.
The god waits there for him. The god invites him to enter.
But, looking through the glowing portal,
he sees on that happy plain not those he thinks wait eagerly for him—
his beloved, his brothers, his companions in war and exile,
all long since dead and gone—
but, sitting pretty and enjoying the gorgeous sunset,
his cousin and bitter enemy, the cause of that war, that exile,
whose arrogance and vicious indolence
plunged the world into grief.
The god informs him that, yes, those he loved have been carried down
the river of fire. Their thirst for justice
offended the cosmic powers, who are jealous of justice.

In their place in the celestial realm, called Alaukika in the ancient texts,
the breaker of faith is now glorified.
He, at least, acted in keeping with his nature.
Who has not felt a little of the despair the son of righteousness now feels,
staring wildly around him?
The god watches, not without compassion and a certain wonder.
This is the final illusion,
the one to which all the others lead.
He has to pierce through it himself, without divine assistance.
He will take a long time about it,
with only his dog to keep him company,
the mongrel dog, celebrated down the millennia,
who has waded with him,
shivered and burned with him,
and never abandoned him to his loneliness.
That dog bears a slight resemblance to my dog,
a skinny, restless, needy, overprotective mutt,
who was rescued from a crack house by Suzanne.
On weekends, and when I can shake free during the week,
I take her to the Long Meadow, in Prospect Park, where dogs
are allowed off the leash in the early morning.
She's gray-muzzled and old now, but you can't tell that by the way she runs.

VIJAY SESHADRI was born in Bangalore, India, in 1954, and came to America as a small child. He grew up in the Midwest and has lived in many parts of the country. His poems and essays have been widely anthologized, and his work has been recognized with a number of honors. He currently lives in Brooklyn and teaches at Sarah Lawrence College.

The Long Meadow has been set in Esprit, a typeface designed by Jovica Veljović, a gifted calligrapher and author of many Latin and Cyrillic faces.

Book design by Wendy Holdman.
Composition by Stanton Publication Services, Inc.
Manufactured by Friesens on acid-free paper.